Dogs in Books

Johannes Rex Anglie genuit

Henrad
Regem
Anglie

Ricardu
Regem
Almanie

Henria

Dogs in Books

A CELEBRATION OF DOG ILLUSTRATION
THROUGH THE AGES

Catherine Britton

THE BRITISH LIBRARY
and
MARK BATTY PUBLISHER

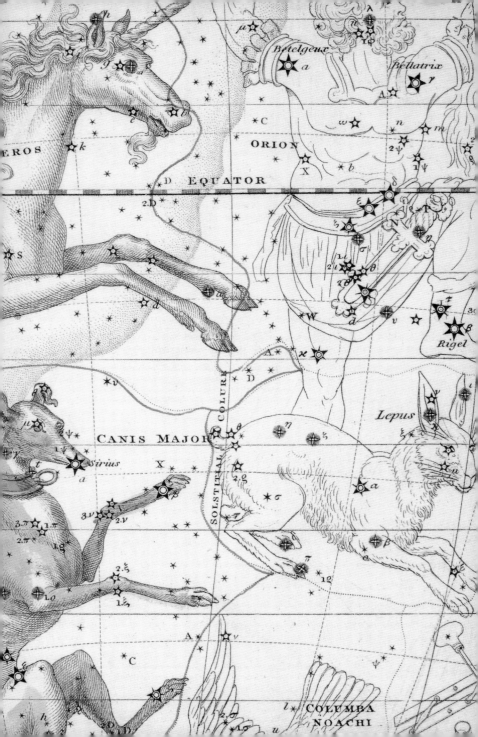

omine ne in fu
rore tuo arguas
me neqz in ira

Introduction

The dog is woven inextricably into our history, art, religion and superstition. Virtually all of the world's cultures assigned the dog a special status, be it as an actual deity such as Anubis the Egyptian dog god, or as a companion to a god, such as Diana, or Artemis, with her hunting hounds.

The written evidence of the relationship between dogs and humans is almost as old as literature itself. In the eighth century BC Homer wrote in *The Odyssey* of Odysseus' return to Ithaca, where only his faithful old dog Argos recognised him. Odysseus had been away, Homer says, for 7300 days, or twenty years, and Argos was by now old and infirm, but still struggled to greet his master:

> He knew his lord; he knew, and strove to meet;
> In vain he strove to crawl and kiss his feet;
> Yet (all he could) his tail, his tears, his eyes,
> Salute his master, and confess his joys.
> (*The Odyssey*, Homer, Book XVII, 360–363, 1811, trans Alexander Pope)

Having made this last gesture of fidelity, Argos then dies, and in a few words, Homer enshrines the literary device of the loyal and subservient dog in the cultural consciousness of western literature:

> The dog, whom Fate had granted to behold
> His lord, when twenty tedious years had roll'd,
> Takes a last look, and having seen him, dies;
> So closed for ever faithful Argos' eyes!
> (*The Odyssey*, Homer, Book XVII, 396–399, 1811, trans Alexander Pope)

Opposite: Illuminated manuscript miniature of
King David with a harp and a dog
From a Book of Hours, circa 1460

The surviving manuscripts from Anglo-Saxon and medieval sources reflect the growing usefulness of the dog in home and working life. A good example is the Luttrell Psalter, a fourteenth century manuscript depicting everyday life in medieval Lincolnshire. Dogs are shown in the margins of the manuscript, in a variety of situations, including baiting bears, jumping through a hoop as part of a street entertainment, fiercely guarding a windmill, and running after and nipping at the heels of an itinerant tradesman as he passes through the village. Other contemporary manuscripts reflected the dog's status in aristocratic and royal households, where greyhounds were illustrated on coats of arms as symbols of fidelity and loyalty, and also used in tombs as the stone 'footstool' in a memorial effigy to the deceased gentry. At about this time the first descriptions for confirmation of a breed start to appear, as dogs belonging to nobility were bred to a standard size and appearance. This was followed in due course by formal and complex rules for hunting and coursing, such as *Countrey Contentments*, written by Gervase Markham and published in 1638, which explained and codified the sport in a way that excluded all but the wealthiest participants.

Shakespeare also recognised the value of a good hunting hound:

LORD: Huntsman, I charge thee, tender well my hounds.
Breathe Merriman—the poor cur is embossed—
And couple Clowder with the deep-mouthed brach.
Saw'st thou not, boy, how Silver made it good
At the hedge-corner, in the coldest fault?
I would not lose the dog for twenty pound.

(*Taming of the Shrew*, Act 1, 12–7)

And Theseus in *A Midsummer Night's Dream* is also very proud of his dogs:

THESEUS: My hounds are bred out of the Spartan kind,
So flewed, so sanded; and their heads are hung
With ears that sweep away the morning dew,
Crook-kneed, and dew-lapped like Thessalian bulls,
Slow in pursuit, but matched in mouth like bells,
Each under each.

(*A Midsummer Night's Dream*, Act 4, Scene 1, 116–21)

However, Shakespeare is not averse to the use of derogatory canine similes and metaphors to portray characters in a negative light. In King Lear, Goneril and Regan are described as 'dog-hearted daughters' and in *The Tempest*, Sebastian curses the Boatswain as their ship is sinking: 'A pox o' your throat, you bawling, blasphemous, incharitable dog!' Dogs are used to highlight King Lear's state of madness when he imagines he hears his dogs barking: 'The little dogs and all, Trey, Blanch, and Sweet-heart, see, they bark at me.' At the end of the play, when Lear's Fool hangs himself, Lear questions why some animals should live whilst his Fool does not:

LEAR: And my poor fool is hang'd! No, no, no life!
Why should a dog, a horse, a rat, have life,
And thou no breath at all?

(*King Lear*, Act 5, Scene 3)

Something bumped violently against the caravan, and shook it from end to end! Was somebody trying to get in?

The importance of the dog is not limited to western writing. Evidence of the Chinese association with the dog dates to the fourth millennium BC when sleeve dogs were bred to fit inside a wealthy owner's garment, and in their astrological literature the dog is honoured as one of the twelve signs of the zodiac. The second day of the Chinese New Year is regarded as the birthday of every dog, and Years of the Dog are 1934, 1946, 1958, 1970, 1982, 1994, 2006, and 2018. If a person is born within the Year of the Dog they are considered to be clever, loyal, resilient, a good listener, and willing to help those in need. Traditionally if a dog comes to your house, you should take it in and look after it as it will bring good fortune – although it should be remembered that the Chinese and Koreans still eat dog meat, so perhaps that situation is not so fortunate for the dog.

In narrative literature, the dog is usually used as a device to illuminate the essential nature of the character. Thus Heathcliff's dogs in *Wuthering Heights* are handsome, taciturn, and vicious when provoked, and Bill Sikes' dog Bull's-eye from *Oliver Twist* is ugly, cruel, and quick to attack. In contrast, there are the many literary dogs who demonstrate extraordinary loyalty and faithfulness to their owners. Often based on true events which were then fictionalised, these stories struck a chord with readers who loved the idea that an animal could be entirely devoted to a human being, even after death. These dog stories featured canines such as Lassie, who travelled home across hundreds of miles after being separated from his owners; Greyfriars Bobby, the Edinburgh dog whose devotion manifested itself through his determination to stay vigilant at his master's grave; and the Japanese Akita

Opposite: Timmy leaps to the rescue
From *Five Go Off in a Caravan* by Enid Blyton, illustrated by Eileen Soper
Hodder and Stoughton, 1959

named Hachiko, who loyally travelled to meet his master's train each evening, long after his owner had passed away.

Whilst these dogs may have been held up as examples of fidelity and loyalty that individuals should themselves strive to achieve, there are plenty of instances of these literary sentiments spilling over into sentimentality. During the nineteenth century this propensity was manifested in both art, such as Landseer, and literature, with authors like Rudyard Kipling – always adept at expressing the concept of unquestioning duty – able to wring the emotion from the page, like with this line from *The Power of a Dog*: 'Buy a pup and your money will buy, Love unflinching that cannot lie.'

In Canada, the story of *Beautiful Joe*, written by Margaret Marshall Saunders and published in 1894, is the tale of a dog who was physically mutilated by his previous owner before finding a happier life with a stable family. It is typical of the animal-rescue literature of the period and was tremendously popular with readers of the time, as was the melodramatically-entitled *The True, Pathetic History of Poor Match* by Holme Lee, published in 1863. It was also common for writers to use small dogs as docile companions to a female protagonist, often to cast them in an unflattering light. Dogs such as Jip, belonging to Dora Spenlow in *David Copperfield*, and Lady Bertram's pug in *Mansfield Park* add to our view of the character in question as decadent and indolent, and the connection between the stifled woman and her pet is striking.

The twentieth century saw the rise of the dog as an equal partner in the characterisation of a work of fiction. Formerly subjected to a lesser role as passive companion to the hero or heroine, it was now an integral part of the plot. Dogs like Timmy, Snowy, and Lassie were just as important as their owners, as they faced dangers and adventures together, frequently coming to each other's rescue – even if the dog was not a natural born adventurer. In illustrated books for younger children the dog is often the sole protagonist, and the story takes place within familiar situations the child can identify such as a garden, birthday party, the park, or the zoo. Illustrated by artists with a strong understanding of graphic design, dogs like Kipper and Spot are composed of simple shapes and bright colours and are drawn against plain white backgrounds; whilst the skeleton dog in the story *Funnybones* by Janet and Allan Ahlberg and published in 1980, goes out on his adventures at night against a black sky, which also maximises the graphic impact of the bony characters. For slightly older children, who are starting to read and understand the story, the rhythm and pace of storytellers such as Lynley Dodd enhance the experience, with perfectly pitched dialogue of her naughty dogs, led by the tearaway Hairy Maclary.

This short book aims to highlight some of the many examples of dogs as they appear in literature, placing them in the context of the history of the period. There are no doubt many favourites that have not been included – it is impossible in a book of this size to include every example – but here are hopefully some of the most famous fictional dogs, which will prompt some memories of the dogs we loved – and continue to love – in our books and in our lives.

Cerberus

Dogs are traditional guardians of the gateways to the underworld. A dog with bared teeth guards the entrance to Takakapsalu in Eskimo mythology, and the Egyptian dog-headed god Anubis was associated with the mummification and journey of the dead to the afterlife. In Greek mythology, Cerberus is the monstrous dog who stands guard at the entrance to the Kingdom of Hades. According to Horace he had a hundred heads, while Hesiod claims he had fifty, but most sources state there were three. He also had a barbed tail, sometimes referred to as that of a dragon, and in some accounts his fur writhes with snakes while he drools black venom from his snarling mouth. When deceased souls entered the underworld a docile Cerberus would let them pass, but once they were there these pitiful shades could never leave.

In Dante's *Inferno* (1307–8) Cerberus was found in the Third Circle of Hell, where he tormented the souls of the gluttonous:

> Over the souls of those submerged beneath
> That mess, is an outlandish, vicious beast,
> His three throats barking, doglike: Cerberus.
> His eyes are blood red; greasy, black, his beard;
> His belly bulges, and his hands are claws;
> His talons tear and flay and render the shades.
> (*Inferno*, Canto VI, 13–18.)

Very few ever managed to overcome such a fierce custodian. In the *Iliad*, Aeneas, with the assistance of the Sibyl calmed Cerberus by feeding him cakes of flour and honey, while Orpheus charmed him with his lyre. Only the mighty Heracles (or Hercules

Opposite: CERBERUS GUARDS THE GATEWAY TO THE UNDERWORLD
From *Archana Deorum* (a commentary on Ovid's *Metamorphoses*)
by Thomas Walsingham, late fifteenth century

in Roman mythology) was able to defeat the creature through physical strength. Heracles had been set a series of twelve tasks, or Labours, by Eurysthemus, the first of which was to kill the lion of Nemea. Its pelt later protected him in his final Labour, when he was ordered to capture Cerberus from the underworld. When Heracles asked Hades for permission to take Cerberus, the grim reply from the underworld's ruler was, 'He is yours if you can master him without chains or arrows'.

Thus constrained, Heracles grabbed the huge dog by its throat, the Nemean lion's pelt defending him from the snapping jaws and barbed tail. Eventually Cerberus choked, enabling Heracles to drag the defeated creature back from the underworld and present him to Eurysthemus. In some other accounts Hercules is not so rough with Cerberus, rendering the dog so surprised by this gentle handling that he allows himself to be led meekly back to the living world.

When Cerberus reached the surface, some of his venom dripped onto the bare rock and the plant aconite sprang up. Also known as wolfsbane, aconite is a traditional protection against werewolves. Another of its names is hecateis, as Hecate (goddess of witches) was the first to use it.

Heracles grabs the collar of Cerberus
From a print by Antonio Tempesta
Nicolas van Aelst, Rome, 1608

Sepe etiam necis illate euidentia canes ad redarguendos
reos indicia prodiderunt ut multo eorum testimonio
plerumqz sit credendum. Antiochie ferunt in remotiore pte ur
bis quendam uirum crepusculo necatum. qui canem sibi ad
uinctum haberet. Miles quidam occisus est astabat canis questu
lacrimabili dni deflebat erumpnam. Mane occurrunt turbe
multe ad spectaculum. Inter quas occurrit et occisor. ut fidem
innocentie faceret. et uelut miserans appropinquit ad
funus. Tunc canis sequestrato paulisp questu doloris
apphendit eum et tenuit. et uelud in eum insultans mi
serabile carm inmurmurans uniuersos conuertit in lac

Dogs in Pliny's Natural History

Pliny the Elder – or, more formally, Gaius Plinius Secundus – had published a number of books before he embarked on his *Historia Naturalis*. Rather than a 'history' in the modern sense of the word, this was more of an encyclopedia encompassing every aspect of the known world. The *Natural History*, dedicated to the emperor Titus, was completed in 77 AD and was, according to Pliny the Younger, the author's nephew, 'a learned and comprehensive work as full of variety as nature itself'.

Book Eight of the *Natural History* is concerned with land animals. It contains descriptions of elephants, camels, crocodiles and hedgehogs as well as mythical creatures such as the basilisk, manticore (a monster with the tail of a scorpion, body of a lion and a man's head) and werewolf. Pliny's description of dogs recognises their loyalty and bravery, as well as offering a 'cure' for the ever-present scourge of rabies:

> The domestic animal that is most faithful
> to man is the dog. Stories are told of the
> faithfulness of dogs: of a dog that fought
> robbers that attacked his master... of a dog
> in Epirus which recognised its master's
> murderer in a crowd and pointed him out
> by barking; of the 200 dogs of the King of
> Garamantes which escorted him home
> from exile and fought anyone who got in
> the way... Only dogs recognise their master,
> know when someone is a stranger, recognise
> their own names, and never forget the way
> to distant places. *(Natural History, Book 8, 61)*

Above: EXAMPLES OF THE FIDELITY OF DOGS AS THEY FIGHT ROBBERS, PROTECT A KING AND TRY TO PUT FOOD IN THE MOUTH OF A DROWNED MAN
From a bestiary, circa thirteenth century

Dogs in the Bible

The dog is not a popular animal in the Bible. Almost all of the forty or so references to the domestic dog are disparaging and even the word is a term of abuse, synonymous with cowardice, laziness and unclean living. 'Why should this dead dog curse my lord the King? Let me go over, I pray thee, and take off his head' (2 Samuel 16:9). Domestic dogs are most commonly described as scavengers, barking and howling outside the city walls at night and of use during the day for only the most unclean tasks. They are described in Exodus as being the best means of destroying refuse and rotting food unfit for human consumption, 'And ye shall be holy men unto me: neither shall ye eat any flesh that is torn of beasts in the field; ye shall cast it to the dogs' (Exodus 22:31), and there is even mention of them devouring human bodies, 'Him that dieth of Jeroboam in the city shall the dogs eat' (1 Kings 14:11).

There are many colourful references to wild dog-like animals in the Bible, such as hyenas, foxes and wolves, but the domestic 'pariah' dog was despised rather than feared. The term is employed as an expression of base humility, 'What is thy servant that thou shouldst look upon such a dead dog as I am' (2 Samuel 9:8), but in more recent years this negative image has been transformed. Pariah dogs have been bred in Israel since the 1930s for military use. Superbly adapted to desert life, they can survive with minimum sustenance and are considered alert and intelligent animals. They have also been trained to be guide dogs for the blind, and the pariah dog is now Israel's national dog.

Opposite: TWO SHEPHERDS AND THEIR SHEEPDOG HEAR OF THE BIRTH OF JESUS
From a fifteenth century Book of Hours, France

Puer natus est nobis

Deus in adiutorium
meum intende.
Domine ad
adiuuandum me festina.

The DOG & the Shadow

IS image the Dog did not
know,
Or his bone's, in the pond's
painted show:
"T'other dog," so he thought,
"Has got more than he ought";
So he snapped, & his dinner
saw go!

·GREED·IS·SOMETIMES·
CAUGHT·BY·ITS·
OWN·BAIT

Above: THE FABLE OF THE DOG WHO THOUGHT HIS REFLECTION
POSSESSED A TASTIER BONE
From *Baby's Own Aesop*, rhymes by W.J. Linton, illustrated by Walter Crane.
Frederick Warne and Co., 1887

Opposite: THE FABLE OF THE THIEF AND HIS DOG. A DOG IS RIGHTLY SUSPICIOUS
WHEN A THIEF ATTEMPTS TO BRIBE HIM WITH FOOD
From *Aesop's Fables*, text by Thomas James, illustrated by John Tenniel.
John Murray, 1848

Aesop's Fables

'A dog who was crossing a river carrying a piece of meat looked down and saw his reflection in the water. Thinking the reflection was another dog with a bigger piece of meat, the dog dropped the meat he had and jumped into the water to take the larger piece, and ended up with no meat at all'.

Very little is known about the life of Aesop. The Greek writer Herodotus (485–25 BC) recorded that he was born a slave around 620 BC. The comedies of Aristophanes (448–388 BC) refer to his fables but, as with Herodotus, both clearly were describing a person who had already been dead for several hundred years. Many of Aesop's fables featured animals and birds often making a mistake or behaving badly and then suffering the consequences. The first printed version of *Aesop's Fables* in English was published in 1484 in London by William Caxton, one of the earliest texts from his printing press. Many others followed, including John Newbery's *Fables in Verse for the Improvement of the Young and the Old* (1757) and the editions of Thomas Bewick, published from his workshops in Newcastle upon Tyne, and distinguished for the

quality of their woodcuts. Some later editions were particularly notable for their illustrations, for example *Aesop's Fables: a new version, chiefly from original sources*, illustrated by John Tenniel, and published by John Murray in 1848. Its success led to John Tenniel's appointment as chief illustrator (with John Leech) on *Punch* magazine, and later by Lewis Carroll for the first printed edition of *Alice in Wonderland*.

Hunting Dogs

For the medieval nobleman, hunting with dogs was a way of life. Together with warfare and courtly love, hunting was a required skill for any man of rank – one in which all kings and members of the aristocracy were expected to excel. The best hunting dogs were given as gifts from one monarch to another, confirming both the status of the owner and the tribute to the recipient, and to honour a distinguished guest one would take them hunting.

A number of medieval breeding and veterinary manuscripts give practical advice for choosing a dog. The highest 'rank' of courtly dog was the greyhound (see the characteristics of a greyhound, p.28). The greyhound is a sight hound, that is, a dog bred to pursue its quarry using its sense of sight rather than smell.

The other dog that was needed to hunt was the alaunt, sometimes referred to as a mastiff. In illustrations it is usually shown as smooth coated like a greyhound, but with a broader and shorter head. Much stronger, it was often used against larger animals such as bears. Alaunts were powerful dogs and hard to control, and are depicted wearing muzzles and sometimes heavy spiked collars. The *Livre du Chasse* by Gaston Phoebus recommends using greyhounds and alaunts together, enabling the swift greyhound to catch the animal first before the alaunt moves in to pull the quarry down with brute force.

Chaucer's *Knight's Tale* describes alaunts as a dog favoured by the king, so much so that they sit by his chair, albeit tightly bound by their muzzles:

Opposite: Huntsmen returning with their dogs
From *The Golf Book*, sixteenth-century Book of Hours by Simon Bening

About his cher ther wenten whyte alaunts,
Twenty and mo, as grete as any stere
To hunten at the leoun or the der,
And folwed him, with mosel fast y-bounde.

Hunting dogs were highly valued, and household accounts show large sums spent on their upkeep. They were not only the preserve of kings. The central character of Chaucer's *Monk's Tale* was also an enthusiastic owner, as described in the Prologue:

Greyhounds he hadde as swifte as fowel in flight;
Of pryking and of hunting for the hare flight;
Was al his lust, for no cost woud he spare.

The dog that to modern eyes is most recognisable as a hunting dog is the scent hound (the antecedent of today's foxhound and beagle) whose powerful instinct to hunt using its sense of smell

enabled them to pursue their quarry over many miles. Medieval hounds were kept in large packs, cared for more diligently than many other members of the household. The huntsman was also expected to be apothecary and surgeon as the dogs were in constant danger of being wounded, and surgical needles were a recurring expense in household accounts. The other great danger was rabies, for which there was no cure. There are records from Paris of payments to the *Varlet de Chiens*:

> to take all the hounds of the King ... and to have
> a Mass sung in the presence of said hounds and
> to offer candles in their sight, for fear of the mal
> de rage, the disease of rabies...
>
> (Perron le Parquier, Ms Fr.7845, Bibliotheque Nationale de France)

Above: A WOMAN RELEASES TWO HOUNDS TO PURSUE A STAG
From the *Smithfield Decretals*, 1310–20

The Greyhound

FROM *Mayster of Game* (c.1272)

The Greihound should have a long hede and
somedele grete, ymaked in the manner of a luce;
a good large mouth and good sessours,
the one again the other, so that the nether
jaws passe not them above, ne that thei
above passe not him neither.
The neck should be grete and long,
and bowed as a swanne's neck.
Her shuldres as a roebuck; the for leggs streght
and gret ynow, and nought to hind legges;
the feet straught and round as a catte, and great
cleas; the boones and the joynetes of the cheyne
grete and hard as the chyne of an hert;
the thighs great and squarred as an hare; the
houghs steight, and not crompyng as of an oxe.
A catte's tayle, making a ring at eend,
but not to hie.
Of all manere of Greihondes there byn
both good and evel;
Natheless the best hewe is rede falow,
with a black moselle.

From *Mayster of Game*, c.1272, by Edward Duke of York, (modern edition ed.
W A and F Baillie-Grohman, Chatto & Windus, London 1904).

Opposite: A HUNTSMAN KEEPS HIS TWO GREYHOUNDS
FIRMLY RESTRAINED WITH A LEASH
From the *Luttrell Psalter*, circa 1320–40

COPYRIGHT
1895
BY E. FISTER

"THE PRINT OF A MAN'S NAKED FOOT IN THE SHORE."

Robinson Crusoe's Dog

Since its first publication in 1719, Daniel Defoe's *Robinson Crusoe* has been a model for many similar tales of survival in primitive conditions and against great odds. Although perceived today as a book for children, it was not intended as such; Daniel Defoe wrote it as a true story, based on the contemporary account of Alexander Selkirk's five years on an uninhabited island. The first edition was published by W Taylor in April 1719, and by the end of the year a further four editions had appeared. The literary genre of shipwreck and survival became popular with many similar stories and spin-offs such as *The Swiss Family Robinson* by Johann Wyss, and *The Dog Crusoe* by R M Ballantyne.

Although Crusoe's dog is barely mentioned in the text, it is widely used in the illustrations. There is no consistency in the way the dog is represented, but as there is no description of him this is not surprising. He also has no name, which is strange, at least to the modern reader, since he was obviously a valued companion. The longest passage is at the beginning of the book when Crusoe is first shipwrecked: '...as for the dog, he jumped out of the ship of himself, and swam on shore to me the day after I went on shore with my first cargo, and was a trusty servant to me many years'.

Opposite: Robinson Crusoe and his dog see the footprint of Man Friday
From the 1895 edition of *The Life and Strange Surprising Adventures of Robinson Crusoe*
by Daniel Defoe, illustrated by Joseph Finnemore,
with G H Thompson and Archibald Webb. Ernest Nister, 1895

Old Mother Hubbard

Until the eighteenth century almost all reading material for children was didactic and moralising. Such books as there were for children were designed to improve and instruct, rather than to entertain. This changed in 1744 with the publication of *Tommy Thumb's Pretty Song book*, a tiny book of thirty-nine rhymes, printed in black and red and published by Mary Cooper in London. The *Song book* is the earliest collection of illustrated nursery rhymes, among them 'Baa, Baa Black Sheep', 'Oranges and Lemons' and 'Bye Baby Bunting'. These rhymes were undoubtedly not new; they had been sung and recited for generations, passed down in the oral tradition. However, this was the first time they had been illustrated and published in a form designed specifically to amuse children.

The nursery rhyme of Old Mother Hubbard appeared in 1805 as *The Comic Adventures of Old Mother Hubbard and her Dog*. It was published by John Harris, who had previously brought out a number of illustrated books for children. The rhyme was already known, possibly as a song, as *The Times* of 17 April 1799 carried an advertisement for a music book entitled *Dr Arnold's New Juvenile Amusements*. It declared that among the rhymes featured were 'Humpty Dumpty', 'Hark the Dogs do Bark' and 'Old Mother Hubbard'. The book was 'to be had of the author, Duke Street, Westminster; or at all the Music Shops'.

The 1805 edition was illustrated by Sarah Catherine Martin, a lady who earlier in her life had turned down a marriage proposal from the future William IV, when he was a naval cadet at Portsmouth and her father was naval commissioner there. She created the illustrations at the behest of her future brother-in-law (to whom the book is dedicated) who was apparently tired of her talking incessantly while he was trying to court her sister.

Whatever the circumstances surrounding its origins, the little book quickly became a fashionable bestseller; ten thousand

Above and overleaf: THE IMPRESSIVE ANTICS OF OLD MOTHER HUBBARD'S DOG,
WRITTEN AND ILLUSTRATED BY SARAH CATHERINE MARTIN
From *The comic adventures of Old Mother Hubbard and her dog*.
John Harris (second edition) 1806

The Dame going to Market
  Was caught in the rain,
He held her Umbrella,
  And She held her train.

She went to the Tavern
For White wine & Red;
When she came back
The Dog stood on his head.

copies were sold at a shilling each. For the 1806 edition (illustrated here) the copper plates were re-engraved and hand-coloured pictures introduced. The dog – nameless, male and of an indeterminate breed – is the most versatile and intelligent of his species, and the manner of tasks he achieves while his mistress is away becomes increasingly impressive and bizarre.

The Musicians of Bremen

Many traditional folk tales include animals who would normally be enemies working together towards a common aim – usually freedom from servitude and the physical comforts of plentiful food and a warm home. The animals in these stories are almost always downtrodden, and unite to outwit, and sometimes physically to overcome, their human masters in order to achieve a better life.

A typical example is *The Musicians of Bremen*. In this story, collected by Jacob and Wilhelm Grimm for the second edition of *Kinder-und Hausmärchen* of 1819, a donkey, dog, cat and cockerel band together to travel to Bremen, where they believe they will find the freedom to live safer lives. They find a house in the woods, but it is occupied by thieves. The animals stand on one another's shoulders and produce a terrible noise, which temporarily scares the robbers away. That night the robbers return, but are confronted by the glowing eyes of the cat, which they mistake for a witch. The dog then bites one of the robbers on the leg, the donkey kicks him, and the cockerel crows. The robbers, believing that the house is possessed by demons, run away for good, so leaving the animals to live in peace. It may be noted, however, that the 'musicians' never actually reach Bremen!

The first editions of *Grimm's Fairy Tales* in 1812 and 1815 were scholarly in style with no pictures, but these were rapidly revised to appeal to a wider readership. In 1823 a London lawyer, Edgar Taylor, saw the tales' potential appeal for a younger audience, and translated them into English. The resulting volume of *German Popular Stories*, with a frontispiece and eleven etchings by George Cruikshank, was the first of many hundreds of versions of the stories. *The Musicians of Bremen* has been interpreted in many forms, including a story by the Muppets, and as a Japanese manga series (the characters appear as punk rock musicians, travelling to Tokyo to become 'Gods of Rock').

A DONKEY, DOG, CAT AND COCKEREL MAKE THEIR OWN FORM OF MUSIC
IN ORDER TO FRIGHTEN AWAY ROBBERS FROM THEIR HOUSE
From *The Fairy Tales of the Brothers Grimm*, translated by Mrs Edgar Lucas,
illustrated by Arthur Rackham. Constable & Co., 1909

The Dogs

FROM *The Tinderbox*

Magical animals are an essential part of many fairy tales, and *The Tinderbox* by Hans Christian Andersen is no exception. A brave soldier is sent by a witch to retrieve a tinder box (a historical version of a match box), hidden inside a hollow tree. Inside the tree are three rooms, and inside them are three chests full of money. Each chest is guarded by a huge dog which the plucky hero must overcome in order to retrieve the riches. In addition to their size and ferocity, each dog has terrible eyes. Those of the first are the size of saucers, the second the size of mill wheels and the third 'as big as the Round Tower of Copenhagen', which 'spun like wheels' when the dog rolled them.

The soldier discovers that by striking the tinderbox he can command these fearsome dogs, and he enlists their powers, firstly to bring him more money, and later on to carry a sleeping princess from her copper castle to the soldier, so that he may kiss her. When the King discovers his daughter has been 'visiting' the soldier, he captures him and sentences him to hang. On the scaffold the soldier strikes the tinderbox and the dogs appear once more. This time they take 'the judges and the council, some by the leg and some by the nose' and throw them up in the air so high that they come down broken to bits. "Don't!" cried the King, but the biggest dog took him and the Queen too and tossed them up after the others.'

The story ends when the soldier marries the Princess, but the conclusion is unsettling: 'The wedding lasted a week, and the three dogs sat at the table, with their eyes opened wider than ever before'.

Opposite: ONE OF THE DOGS FROM THE TINDERBOX
CARRIES THE SLEEPING PRINCESS TO THE SOLDIER
From *Hans Andersen's Fairy Tales*, illustrated by Frank C Papé.
Dutton & Co., 1910

The Tinderbox is one of Andersen's earliest stories. It unusually contains elements of two older folk tales, *The Blue Light* and *The Three Dogs*, both collected earlier by the Brothers Grimm. At first the story seems quite conventional: the brave soldier finds wealth, rescues a princess from the castle and marries her. But Andersen's tale is subversive: the soldier kills the witch who has helped him find the treasure, and then squanders his money; he kidnaps the princess and orders the murder of her parents. Instead of the usual 'happy ever after' conclusion, the abiding, ominous image for the reader is of three monstrous dogs, sitting at the wedding table, watching over the guests at the feast.

The story was first published by C A Reitzel in Copenhagen in May 1835. A cheap, sixty-one page collection of three fairy tales, it was entitled *Fairy Tales for Children, First Collection* (or *Eventyr, fortalte for Børn, Første Samling* in the original Danish), and followed by a second collection in December of that year, and a third in 1836. The three collections were then brought out in one volume, but it was not until the publication of 'The Little Mermaid' in 1838 that Andersen found the success and recognition he craved.

Amongst the finest editions of Andersen's stories is the 1916 volume published in London by George Harrap. He commissioned the illustrator Harry Clarke (1889–1931) to create sixteen colour plates and twenty line drawings, and although Clarke's artwork sometimes fails to follow the details of the story, it is hard to disagree with Harrap's view that 'Harry Clarke interpreted the immortal tales with an imagination which penetrated the heart of his subjects and transmuted them into shining gold'.

Opposite: THE SOLDIER IS TAKEN ABACK BY THE SIGHT OF
THE SUPERNATURAL DOG STANDING ON THE CHEST OF MONEY
From *Fairy Tales* by Hans Christian Andersen, illustrated by Harry Clarke.
G G Harrap & Co., 1916

BULL'S-EYE FOLLOWS BILL SIKES ACROSS THE ROOFTOPS OF LONDON
From *Oliver Twist* by Charles Dickens, illustrated by George Cruikshank.
Chapman and Hall, 1902

Bull's-eye

FROM *Oliver Twist*

A white shaggy dog, with his face scratched and torn in twenty different places, skulked into the room.

"Why didn't you come in afore?" said the man. "You're getting too proud to own me afore company, are you? Lie down!"

This command was accompanied with a kick, which sent the animal to the other end of the room. He appeared well used to it, however; for he coiled himself up in a corner very quietly, without uttering a sound, and winking his very ill-looking eyes twenty times in a minute, appeared to occupy himself in taking a survey of the apartment.

There was a long pause. Every member of the respectable coterie appeared plunged in his own reflections; not excepting the dog, who by a certain malicious licking of his lips seemed to be meditating an attack upon the legs of the first gentleman or lady he might encounter in the streets when he went out.

Bull's-eye is the English bull terrier companion of the evil character Bill Sikes. A rare example of an out-and-out 'bad' dog, his viciousness mirrors Sikes' animal-like brutality, while Sikes' violence is evident in the dog's appearance. The noble canine characteristics of loyalty and obedience are cruelly distorted, as the dog is willing to harm anyone on Sikes' whim.

After Sikes has murdered Nancy, however, Bull's-eye leaves bloody paw prints on the floor of her room. Sikes becomes determined to get rid of the dog, seeing him as evidence of his own guilt and convinced that he will give him away. Eventually the law catches up with Sikes, and Bull's-eye also meets his inevitable bloody end. As Sikes hangs dead, suspended in the mechanism of a crane above a muddy creek, Bull's-eye appears: 'With a dismal howl, the dog, which had been concealed until now, ran backwards and forwards on the parapet before, collecting himself with a spring, he jumped for the dead man's shoulders. Missing his aim, he fell into the ditch and, turning

completely as he went, dashed out his brains'.

Oliver Twist was Dickens' second novel. The central theme of the book is a scathing attack on the New Poor Law, which had replaced the old system of parish relief for the poor with a brutal workhouse regime. Dickens' first child had been born in January 1837 and, with a newborn baby at home, he threw himself into the story of an innocent child's struggle in the nightmarish world of London's overcrowded slums.

Some of his readers were taken aback by the novel's dark tone. The British Prime Minister Lord Melbourne was openly disgusted by its portrayal of low life, and even advised Queen Victoria not to read the book, saying it dealt with 'paupers, criminals and other unpleasant subjects'. The Queen found the novel 'excessively interesting', however, and the book remains one of Dickens' most popular and frequently dramatised works.

BULL'S-EYE COWERS IN THE CORNER UNDER
THE MALEVOLENT GAZE OF BILL SIKES
From *Oliver Twist* by Charles Dickens,
illustrated by Fred Barnard, 1836–7

Tray

FROM *Struwwelpeter*

Some book concepts evolve through a long period of gestation, while others arise in a moment – often borne of necessity. Such was the case with Dr Heinrich Hoffman of Frankfurt, who in December 1844 went to buy a picture book as a Christmas present for his young son. He was not impressed by the choice available: 'What did I find? Long tales, stupid collections of pictures, moralizing stories, beginning and ending with admonitions like, "The child must be truthful" or "Children must be kept clean"'.

The disgruntled Hoffmann purchased a blank exercise book and proceeded to compose five cautionary stories in verse, illustrating them himself. The last tale in the book was the story of 'Struwwelpeter' (shock-headed Peter), a slovenly boy whose name provided the title of later editions. Hoffmann's collection, published in 1845, went on to become the most famous German children's book ever published.

Each story involves grotesque exaggerations of the consequences of bad behaviour. Harriet, for example, who plays with matches, is burnt to ashes. Thumb-sucking Conrad is confronted by 'a great, long, red-legged scissor man' who snips off his thumbs. The brutal Frederick, who tortures and kills small creatures, whips his dog Tray until the animal finally turns and bites him. Frederick then has to take 'nasty physic' while Tray takes on a life of privilege, sitting in Frederick's chair, and eating his sausage supper. The whip with which the dog was beaten hangs over the back of the chair, symbolising the reversal of power between the two protagonists.

Opposite: FREDERICK LIES INJURED IN BED WHILST HIS DOG TRAY SITS DOWNSTAIRS EATING SAUSAGES.
From *Der Struwwelpeter, oder lustige Geschichten und drollige Bilder für Kinder von 3-6 Jahren*, written and illustrated by Heinrich Hoffmann, Frankfurt, 1876

In's Bett muß Friedrich nun hinein,
Litt vielen Schmerz an seinem Bein;
Und der Herr Doctor sitzt dabei
Und gibt ihm bitt're Arzenei.

Der Hund an Friedrichs Tischchen saß,
Wo er den großen Kuchen aß;
Aß auch die gute Leberwurst
Und trank den Wein für seinen Durst.
Die Peitsche hat er mitgebracht
Und nimmt sie sorglich sehr in Acht.

Am Brunnen stand ein großer Hund,
Trank Waſſer dort mit ſeinem Mund.
Da mit der Peitſch' herzu ſich ſchlich
Der bitterböſe Friederich;
Und ſchlug den Hund, der heulte ſehr,
Und trat und ſchlug ihn immer mehr.
Da biß der Hund ihn in das Bein,
Recht tief bis in das Blut hinein.
Der bitterböſe Friederich,
Der ſchrie und weinte bitterlich. —
Jedoch nach Hauſe lief der Hund
Und trug die Peitſche in dem Mund.

In Hoffmann's original German text the nameless dog is described simply as 'ein Grosser Hund'. The English edition gives him a name, Tray, and presents him as 'good' and 'faithful', as if to underline the emotional connection between the dog and his master. Tray was a popular name for dogs at that time. An American folk song of 1853 is known as 'Old Dog Tray', and the name also appears in the sentimental poem 'My Dog Tray' (from *Aunt Louisa's London Toy Book* of 1890).

In the earliest versions of the *Struwwelpeter* story, the illustrations are subtle and delicate. Intricate details of the dog, such as his tail and collar, are carefully picked out. However the pictures became simplified in later versions and the detail was lost. In the illustrations from the fourth English edition the style has become quite crude: figures are simplified, and blood spurts dramatically from Frederick's leg as Tray bites him. By the time of the edition of *Struwwelpeter* reproduced in the present English language edition, the colours have degraded into harsh acidic tones, while the drawings of Tray have simplified even further into the most basic cartoon dog.

Opposite: TRAY DRINKS FROM THE TROUGH BEFORE BEING WHIPPED
BY FREDERICK AND TAKES REVENGE BY BITING HIS LEG
From *Der Struwwelpeter, oder lustige Geschichten und drollige Bilder für Kinder von
3–6 Jahren*, written and illustrated by Heinrich Hoffmann.

Above: THE SAME SEQUENCE OF EVENTS FROM AN EARLY ENGLISH EDITION
Note the cruder style of illustration.
From *The English Struwwelpeter, or pretty stories and funny pictures for little children*,
anonymous translation, illustrator unknown

Edward Lear

Quintessentially English, with a strong sense of the bizarre, Edward Lear's work continues to amuse and delight, influencing comedians such as Spike Milligan and Ricky Gervais. Originally a painter of ornithology and landscape painting, Lear made his name in 1832 with *Illustrations of the Family of Psittacidae, or Parrots*, one of the finest books of bird illustration ever produced. He was only nineteen years old.

Largely self-taught, Lear composed some nonsense verses and drawings to amuse the children of his patron, the Earl of Derby, which were published by a print-seller, Thomas McLean,

There was an Old Man of Leghorn, the smallest that ever was born ;
But quickly snapt up he was once by a Puppy,
Who devoured that Old Man of Leghorn.

in 1846. They sold reasonably well, mostly to upper-class households who were already customers of McLean. It was not until *The Book of Nonsense* was revised, re-drawn and expanded fifteen years later that it really captured the public imagination, and was subsequently published by Routledge, Warne and Routledge. Lear's narrative nonsensical verses (he never called them limericks) were designed to be read aloud, and played upon the rhythms of the speaking voice. He combined the poems with line drawings of figures with enlarged heads, as well as animals, birds and other creatures, recognisable despite their outrageous context.

Above and opposite: BIZARRE DOGS (AND THEIR EQUALLY ODD OWNERS)
FROM THE LIMERICKS OF EDWARD LEAR
From *The Book of Nonsense* written and illustrated by Edward Lear.
Frederick Warne & Co., 1885

There was a Young Lady of Ryde, whose shoe-strings were seldom untied;
She purchased some clogs, and some small spotty Dogs,
And frequently walked about Ryde.

There was an Old Man of Kamschatka, who possessed a remarkably fat Cur;
His gait and his waddle were held as a model
To all the fat dogs in Kamschatka.

The Dear Little Puppy

FROM *Alice in Wonderland*

The task of illustrating *Alice in Wonderland* has been described as 'a sort of illustrators' Everest'. Since the original book was published in 1865, hundreds of artists have attempted to capture the essence of this beguiling story.

The original manuscript by Lewis Carroll (whose actual name was Charles Lutwidge Dodgson) was presented to Alice Liddell, daughter of the Dean of Christ Church College, Oxford, where Dodgson lectured in mathematics. His friends urged him to publish the manuscript, so he revised and expanded the work, engaging an illustrator, John Tenniel, to create the pictures. Tenniel was well established as a cartoonist for *Punch* magazine, but it was his animal drawings for an edition of *Aesop's Fables* that had caught Dodgson's eye. The result of their partnership was the first printed edition of *Alice in Wonderland*: a brilliant combination of Dodgson's surreal, often illogical, text with Tenniel's detailed drawings.

The puppy does not appear in the original Alice manuscript. He was one of the animals created for the printed edition and exists as a minor character, devised to emphasise Alice's vulnerability when she shrinks in size after eating some pebbles: 'An enormous puppy was looking down at her with large round eyes, and feebly stretching out his paw, trying to touch her. "Poor little thing!" said Alice in a coaxing tone, and she tried hard to whistle to it, but she was terribly frightened all the time at the thought that it might be hungry, in which case it would be very likely to eat her up'.

Alice in Wonderland was an immediate success. It was followed in 1871 by *Alice Through the Looking Glass*, and in 1890 by *The Nursery*

Opposite: THE 'DEAR LITTLE PUPPY' TOWERS OVER ALICE
From *The Nursery Alice* by Lewis Carroll, illustrated by John Tenniel.
Macmillan & Co., 1890

came forwards to meet them, keeping his
musket pointed straight at Bruno, who stood
quite still, though he turned pale and kept tight
hold of Sylvie's hand, while the Sentinel walked
solemnly round and round them, and looked at
them from all points of view.

"Oobooh, hooh boohooyah!" He growled
at last. "Woobah yahwah oobooh! Bow
wahbah woobooyah? Bow wow?" he asked
Bruno, severely.

Alice. This shortened and adapted version, designed to meet the needs of a younger audience, featured twenty colour illustrations, the only *Alice* images that Tenniel ever coloured. In Chapter Six, 'The Dear Little Puppy', Dodgson seeks to reassure his young readers of the puppy's innocence and lack of malice towards Alice:

> So it really was a little Puppy, you see. And isn't it a little pet? And look at the way it's barking at the little stick that Alice is holding out for it! You can see she was a little afraid of it, all the time, because she's got behind that great thistle, for fear it should run over her. That would have been just about as bad, for her, as it would be for you to be run over by a waggon and four horses!

He then goes on to compare the puppy to another dog called Dash, which has led some to assume that the puppy in *Alice* is also called Dash. The puppy is nameless, however, and of all the animals and creatures in *Alice* it is the only one that never speaks.

Dogs also featured in *Sylvie and Bruno*, in which two children visit Dogland, a country ruled by a Newfoundland dog who is not altogether happy with royal protocol: 'It's quite a relief getting away from that Palace now and then! Royal dogs have a dull life, I can tell you!'

Opposite: 'A MASTIFF, DRESSED IN A SCARLET COLLAR, AND CARRYING A MUSKET, WAS PACING UP AND DOWN, LIKE A SENTINEL, IN FRONT OF THE ENTRANCE'.
From *Sylvie and Bruno* by Lewis Carroll, illustrated by Harry Furniss.
Macmillan & Co., 1889

" You ought to be ashamed of yourself!"

TOTO LOOKS ON WITH SOME INTEREST AS DOROTHY TALKS TO THE COWARDLY LION
From *The New Wizard of Oz* by L. Frank Baum illustrated by W W Denslow.
Bobbs-Merrill Co, 1903

Toto

FROM *The Wonderful Wizard of Oz*

'I'll get you my pretty, and your little dog too!'
The Wicked Witch of the West, *The Wonderful Wizard of Oz*

Toto is Dorothy's dog in the Oz series of books,

introduced at the beginning of the first book as having 'saved her from going as gray as her surroundings'. He is 'a little black dog, with long silky hair and small black eyes that twinkled merrily on either side of his funny, wee nose', and was drawn as a Cairn, or possibly a Yorkshire terrier. In the first book Toto behaves very much as an ordinary dog: when the cyclone approaches their house in Kansas he runs and hides under the bed; when Dorothy meets the scarecrow he runs around barking, and later on he tries to bite the leg of the tin man, 'which hurt his teeth'. Toto is also a 'real' dog in that he does not speak, although he gains this ability in later Oz books. He is crucially important to the story. When Dorothy and her friends are finally granted an audience with the Wizard in the Emerald City, it is Toto who knocks over a wooden screen to reveal the very ordinary man behind it.

Although Toto is an integral part of the printed books, and of the famous 1939 film, his importance to other versions of the story has been varied. In the 1902 stage version of the story, for example, Toto was replaced by a cow called Imogene, and for most of the 1985 film *Return to Oz* he is usurped as Dorothy's companion by Billina the chicken. Famously, Terry, the (female) Cairn terrier who played Toto in the 1939 film, was paid $125 per week – far more than the $50 weekly salary for the Munchkins.

L Frank Baum had written a number of moderately successful books for both adults and children before striking gold with a collection of children's poems entitled *Father Goose, His Book*. The illustrations were by W W Denslow, a commercial artist with a flair for art poster designs popular in the 1890s, and *Father Goose* became the bestselling children's picture book of 1899. As a

result George M Hill, Baum and Denslow's publisher, was keen to produce anything new they had created, and *The Wonderful Wizard of Oz* was published in 1900. It was a bestseller from the start, and over 10,000 copies were sold within two weeks of publication. Hill's fortunes were unable to match those of the book, however, and he was declared bankrupt in 1901. After a complicated period of financial and legal wrangling, a second edition of the book was published in 1903 by Bobbs-Merrill as *The New Wizard of Oz*, which was shortened on the second printing to the now-familiar version called *The Wizard of Oz*.

L Frank Baum went on to write a further thirteen Oz books, although none matched the success of the first. It is estimated that by the time *The Wizard of Oz* came into (US) public domain in 1956, there were over three million copies in print.

Left: Dorothy clings on to Toto as
the tornado carries them off to Oz
From *The New Wizard of Oz* by L Frank Baum,
illustrated by W W Denslow.
Bobbs-Merrill Co., 1903

The Hound of the Baskervilles

Ghostly dogs are not unusual in literature, particularly in traditional folk tales. Just as chains clank and winds moan, so the ghostly howl of a dog is a common feature of ghost stories, usually as the precursor to death and disaster. In England one of the most famous phantom dogs is Black Shuck, said to prowl the East Anglian countryside; anyone who looks into his eyes is certain to die within the year. Another enduring legend is that of the Barguest, a mythical hellhound said to haunt the Yorkshire Dales.

Arthur Conan Doyle was certainly aware of these stories when he decided to take a golfing holiday in the seaside resort of Cromer in Norfolk in 1901. During his visit Conan Doyle had dinner with Benjamin Bond Cabell at Cromer Hall, and heard the story of Cabell's ancestor, Richard Cabell – Lord of Brook Manor and Buckfastleigh in Devon – who had supposedly been killed by a monstrous dog. According to the story, Cabell's wife had supposedly been unfaithful; after an argument with her husband, she fled out on to Dartmoor. Cabell pursued her and stabbed her, but as he committed the murder his wife's faithful dog attacked him, tearing out his throat. The ghost of the dog was said to haunt Dartmoor and to reappear to each generation of the Cabell family. It is clear that Richard Cabell became the model for the evil Hugo Baskerville in Conan Doyle's classic tale.

The finished story of *The Hound of the Baskervilles* was published in *The Strand* magazine between August 1901 and April 1902. At this point there had been no new Sherlock Holmes stories for almost eight years, as the great detective had apparently met his end at the Reichenbach Falls in 1893, but Conan Doyle knew he

Opposite: THE CURSE OF THE BASKERVILLES
From *The Hound of the Baskervilles* by Arthur Conan Doyle, illustrated by Sidney Paget.
Strand magazine, serialized 1901–1902 .

THE HOUND OF THE BASKERVILLES.

(*See page* 128.)

"THE HOUND OF THE BASKERVILLES."

(*See page* 252.)

had a strong story, and what he described as 'a real creeper': 'A hound it was, an enormous coal-black hound, but not such a hound as mortal eyes have ever seen. Fire burst from its open mouth, its eyes glowed with a smouldering glare, its muzzle and hackles and dewlap were outlined in flickering flame. Never in the delirious dream of a disordered brain could anything more savage, more appalling, more hellish be conceived than that dark form and savage face'.

The story was an immediate success, and the circulation of *The Strand* magazine rose by 30 percent. The illustrations were by Sidney Paget, although there is some evidence to suggest that *The Strand* thought they had commissioned his brother Walter, an illustrator known for his work on *Treasure Island* and *Robinson Crusoe*. Conan Doyle did not wholly approve of the result, saying that he had made Sherlock Holmes much handsomer than he wanted. Whatever the circumstances, the story of the terrifying devil dog became embedded in the public consciousness, where it has remained ever since. Drawing on age-old fears of darkness, lonely places and wild beasts, *The Hound of the Baskervilles* is probably Conan Doyle's most famous story.

Opposite: HOLMES AND WATSON SEE THE GHOSTLY HOUND, 'OUTLINED IN FLICKERING FLAME'.

Above: THE HOUND CLAIMS ANOTHER VICTIM
From *The Hound of the Baskervilles* by Arthur Conan Doyle, illustrated by Sidney Paget. *Strand* magazine, serialized 1901–1902

Buck and White Fang

FROM *The Call of the Wild* and *White Fang*

At the end of the nineteenth century Jack London, along with many thousands of eager prospectors, was in the Yukon Territory in the United States seeking his fortune in the Klondike Gold Rush. The brutal conditions he experienced there shaped his outlook and writing, helping him to develop a genre of literary realism and naturalism which in turn tapped into the Darwinian theories of 'survival of the fittest'. Written over just two months in 1902, *The Call of the Wild* is the story of the dog Buck, the offspring of a St Bernard and a shepherd dog who, just like the author, travels from California to follow the Yukon River Trail. Like London, Buck nearly dies in the Northland, but through courage, skill and physical strength he overcomes many setbacks and ends the story triumphant. The story's authenticity resonated with reading public and, after years of failure as a writer, London found critical acclaim:

> *Fierce, brutal, splashed with blood, and alive with the crack of the whip and the blow of the club*
> (San Francisco Chronicle, August 1903).
> *Not a pretty story at all, but a very powerful one*
> (Atlantic Monthly, November 1903).

However, London's financial acumen did not match his literary success. In a pattern that was to recur throughout his career, he undersold his work, charging $750 for serial rights in the *Saturday Evening Post* and $2000 for book rights to Macmillan. Two years later he wrote *White Fang*, in many ways a mirror to *Call of the Wild*, in which a wolf (actually the son of a half-breed) learns to love and trust his master. *White Fang* explores the same themes of man and beast facing nature at its cruellest, and although some-times regarded as a lesser work it is still an immensely powerful read.

THE COVER OF *THE CALL OF THE WILD*
illustrated by Philip R Goodwin and Charles Livingston Bull.
William Heinemann, 1903

Aileen

FROM *A Dog's Tale*

Mark Twain's *A Dog's Tale* was written in 1903, many years after the success of *The Adventures of Tom Sawyer* (1876) and *The Adventures of Huckleberry Finn* (1884). Written by Twain in support of his daughter Jean's condemnation of vivisection, it is a disturbing tale of the 'rewards' for an animal's loyalty to human beings. The story is told in the voice of the dog, Aileen, and begins in Twain's characteristically wry style: 'My father was a St Bernard, my mother was a collie, but I am a Presbyterian'.

Aileen lives with the wealthy Gray family, and is happy until the day Mr Gray sees her dragging their baby across the hallway, not realising the dog has just rescued the child from a nursery fire. He beats the dog, breaking her leg, although when her heroism is discovered she is treated better than ever, and her happiness seems complete with the birth of a puppy. This idyllic state is not to last: Mr Gray is a neural scientist and experiments on the puppy, blinding it, and the creature dies in great pain. The story ends with Aileen keeping vigil at the puppy's grave, the implication clear that she will die of a broken heart: 'I have watched two whole weeks … I cannot eat, though the servants bring me the best of food … And I am so weak, I cannot stand on my feet anymore'.

A Dog's Tale first appeared in the US in *Harper's Magazine* in December 1903, and in book format in September 1904 published by Harper & Row, and illustrated by the prolific artist and illustrator W G Smedley. Although the critical response was that the story was overly melodramatic and sentimental, it was popular with the reading public, and it remains an interesting example of a work told in a dog's own voice.

Opposite: AFTER HER PUPPY'S DEATH,
THE DOG AILEEN IS COMFORTED BY A SERVANT
From *A Dog's Tale* by Mark Twain, illlustrated by W G Smedley.
Harper & Brothers, 1904

— 67 —

Ginger and Pickles

FROM *The Tale of Ginger and Pickles*

An unusual business partnership between a cat and a dog forms the basis of Beatrix Potter's 1909 book *The Tale of Ginger and Pickles*. The yellow tom-cat Ginger and the smooth-coated fox terrier Pickles set up a small village shop to sell a variety of household provisions such as 'red spotty pocket-handkerchiefs at a penny three farthings'. At first their business goes well, but they make the elementary mistake of offering unlimited credit to their customers. Economic reality prevails, and as their customers fail to repay their debts, the business soon goes bust. There is a happy ending of sorts as Ginger retires and Pickles takes up an alternative career as a gamekeeper.

The story carefully balances the charming domesticity of village life with an uncompromising portrayal of retail economics. The importance of limiting a credit arrangement was (and is) familiar to anyone with any knowledge of running a business. An unsubstantiated rumour claims that Margaret Thatcher described *The Tale of Ginger and Pickles* as the only business book worth reading.

Potter set her story in a real shop in the village of Sawrey in the English Lake District and presented the work as a Christmas present to Louie Warne, the daughter of her publisher Harold Warne, in 1908. The familiar small format edition first appeared in 1930.

In common with the characters in her other books, the animals in this story all wear clothing and behave as humans do – although they are thankfully not completely divorced from realistic animal behaviour. Ginger, for example, 'always asked Pickles to serve the mice as they made his mouth water' while the rabbit customers, understandably, 'were always a little afraid of Pickles'.

PICKLES TAKES A GROCERY ORDER FROM MRS TIGGYWINKLE
From *The Tale of Ginger and Pickles*, written and illustrated by Beatrix Potter.
Frederick Warne & Co., 1909

A palpitating vacuum-cleaner.

the price? You don't expect me to sanction dawgs 'ere for nothin'? Come *on*! It's all found money for you.'

Rudyard Kipling's Dogs

The common themes of loyalty, stoicism and (un-questioning) deference which suffuse much of Kipling's work are evident in his stories and poems about dogs. Perhaps the best known is 'The Power of the Dog', a frequently quoted, unashamedly sentimental poem which first appeared in the collection *Actions and Reactions*. Published in October 1909, the book sold for six-pence in Britain (where it had a print run of 20,000 copies) and $1.50 in America:

> There is sorrow enough in the natural way
> From men and women to fill our day;
> And when we are certain of sorrow in store,
> Why do we always arrange for more?
> Brothers and sisters, I bid you beware
> Of giving your heart to a dog to tear.

Kipling's other, very famous dog appears in the *Just So Stories* in the story of 'The Cat That Walked by Himself'. The Wild Dog is the first of the wild animals to befriend humans, having been attracted to their cave by the smell of roasting meat. The Woman then gives him the mutton bone, and says: 'Wild Thing out of the Wild Woods, help my Man to hunt through the day and guard this Cave at night, and I will give you as many roast bones as you need'.

Opposite: DINAH THE ABERDEEN TERRIER
BARKS AT 'A PALPITATING VACUUM CLEANER'.
From *Collected Dog Stories* by Rudyard Kipling, illustrated by Marguerite Kirmse.
Macmillan & Co., 1934

The dog immediately agrees to this proposal, and thus becomes domesticated: 'When the Man waked up he said, "What is Wild Dog doing here?" And the Woman said, "His name is not Wild Dog any more, but the First Friend, because he will be our friend for always and always and always. Take him with you when you go hunting"'.

Published in September 1902, *Just So Stories* was the only one of his books that Kipling illustrated himself. It has become one of the great classic books of children's literature, selling millions of copies and going through many adaptations.

Dogs are featured in many of Kipling's short stories. 'Garm, a Hostage' (published with *The Power of the Dog* in *Actions and Reactions*) is the story of a bull terrier belonging to an English soldier in India. Garm is given away, and subsequently both he and his original owner decline in health until they are at last reunited. In the final scene they 'rolled on the ground together, shouting and yelping, and hugging. I could not tell which was dog, and which was man'.

Kipling used some of his own favourite dogs in his later short stories. In 'Thy Servant a Dog, The Great Play Hunt' and 'Toby Dog' (published in 1930 under the title of the first story), the narrative is presented in the voice of the dog Boots – modelled on Kipling's own Aberdeen terriers, Wop and James. The simplified vocabulary and dialect are sometimes awkward, although Kipling writes so skillfully that the reader understands what is happening, even though the dog narrator may not. The stories were illustrated by George Loraine Stampa, a cartoonist for *Punch* magazine, who also illustrated Kipling's 1938 *Collected Dog Stories*. As well as the canine illustrations for Kipling, Stampa illustrated Joe Walker's *My Dog and Yours* (1929) and *That Dog of Mine* (1930). He also compiled and illustrated the anthology *In Praise of Dogs* (1948).

Opposite: (below) TEEM THE TREASURE HUNTER AND
(above) GARM THE INDIAN BULL TERRIER

Above: ABLE SEA DOG MALACHI FINDS THE WARMEST SPOT ON BOARD SHIP
From *Collected Dog Stories* by Rudyard Kipling, illustrated by Marguerite Kirmse.
Macmillan & Co., 1934

Snowy

Tintin's fox terrier, Snowy, has loyally accompanied him from his very first adventure (in the Soviet Union in 1929), sharing adventures around the world. Snowy fears nothing except spiders, and generally behaves like most of his kind, sniffing, chasing, biting, barking and eating as much as he can – from a whole chicken in *Red Rackham's Treasure* to a huge bone from a Yeti's cave in *Tintin in Tibet*.

Only in the English language versions of the books is Tintin's dog is known as Snowy. In the original French editions he was named Milou, after Hergé's first girlfriend, leading to some speculation as to whether Snowy may in fact be female. However, Snowy's physical behaviour, especially his habit of cocking his leg, as well as his bragging and swaggering behaviour suggest otherwise. The use of the masculine 'il' in the original French text also seems to indicate that Snowy is definitely a chap.

Despite his obvious doggy persona, Snowy is able to think and speak like a human, although only Tintin can converse with him. He refers on occasion to the Bible and the stories of Conan Doyle (for example in comparing Tintin to Sherlock Holmes); he also

displays geographical knowledge of Egypt in *Cigars of the Pharaoh.*

The fox terrier breed is renowned for its courage and intelligence, characteristics that Snowy frequently displays. He boldly embarks on fights with bigger dogs and even large animals such as lions and gorillas, and his heroism is even more evident when his master is in danger. Snowy rescues Tintin from numerous perilous situations in which canine traits are essential. For example, Snowy can cock his leg to put out a burning fuse, lick Tintin's face to revive him from unconsciousness and, most frequently, direct a well-placed bite into any villainous leg or backside. Even when placed in the most dangerous situation, Snowy looks on the bright side. He is captured by a condor in *Prisoners of the Sun* and carried away to its cliff-top nest; on finding it ominously full of bones, he simply remarks, 'I say, these birds certainly know how to treat a guest!' Such optimism and bravery make Snowy one of literature's great canine heroes, as well-loved by today's readers as by his original audience.

Above: Tintin and Snowy peruse an intriguing letter
From *The Secret of the Unicorn* written and illustrated by Georges Hergé. Casterman, 1943. English edition published by Methuen, 1959

Left: Snowy gets altitude sickness
From *Tintin in Tibet* written and illustrated by Georges Hergé. Casterman, 1960. English edition published by Methuen, 1962

Lassie

The many films, comics, television and radio series about this rough-haired collie all began with one book: *Lassie Come-Home*, published in 1938. The story recounts Lassie's separation from an impoverished Yorkshire family, forced to sell her to a Scottish duke, and describes how Lassie, against all odds, finds her way back to them.

Stories of dogs travelling great distances to be reunited with their owners are not new. The novelist Victor Hugo claimed to have given away his poodle, Baron, to a Russian count when he visited Moscow in 1872. 'To my astonishment', he recalled, 'some months later Baron, alone, but determined, walked from the count's country house outside Moscow, to Paris. There was a joyful reunion for us both'.

A later journey, supported by more substantial evidence and almost certainly the precedent for *Lassie Come-Home*, took place in America in 1924. Bobbie, a three-year-old collie, became separated from his owners while they were on holiday in Indiana. He embarked on a 3000-mile trek back to Oregon, taking six months and travelling through the depths of winter. The story made headlines across America, and many people subsequently came forward to say that they had fed or housed Bobbie on his way home.

It seems quite likely that this story was known to Eric Knight, an English journalist who owned a rough-haired collie and worked in Pennsylvania in the 1930s. Knight, strongly influenced by a Yorkshire upbringing, was particularly driven by the injustice he witnessed when miners were laid off and families forced to sell their belongings. His previous two novels had drawn heavily

Opposite: THE UNMISTAKABLE FEATURES OF LASSIE
From *Lassie Come-Home* by Eric Knight, illustrated by Marguerite Kirmse.
J C Winston Co., 1940

on this background, and in late 1938 *Lassie Come-Home* was published as a novella in the US newspaper *Saturday Evening Post*. Within a year Knight had extended the story into a full-length novel, and from this point the book became a bestseller.

The source of the name Lassie is unclear. She may have been named for a collie who saved a seaman's life in 1915, after the battleship HMS *Formidable* was sunk while on exercises in the English Channel. Over 500 lives were lost, and some of the recovered bodies were laid out in a pub in Lyme Regis. The pub's resident dog, a collie called Lassie, went over to one of the 'corpses' and began to lick his face, whereupon it was realised that the man was still alive.

Whatever the source of the name, Lassie the brand was unstoppable. The studio MGM acquired film rights, and the 1942 film starred Roddy McDowall and Elizabeth Taylor in her second film role. A further six Lassie films followed, followed by radio shows, cartoon strips, and in 1954 the story transferred to television, with an epic 675 episodes. The reworking of the original story of a boy and his dog, united by love and bravery, provided endless sources of dramatic rescues in which the super-intelligent Lassie intervenes to prevent disaster.

In the late 1980s an attempt was made to reinvigorate the stories with *The New Lassie*, notably providing the televison screen debut of a young Leonardo DiCaprio. A Japanese animated

version of the story was made in 1996 as *Meiken Rasshi* (*Famous Dog Lassie*). The story came full circle with the British film of *Lassie*, released in 2005. Faithful to the original story and dialogue, it was the latest – but almost certainly not the last – adaptation of the story of this iconic dog.

Above: LASSIE LEAPS TO FREEDOM
From *Lassie Come-Home* by Eric Knight, illustrated by Marguerite Kirmse.
J C Winston Co., 1940

Cecil Aldin's Dogs

Very few animals have had an obituary published in *The Times*, but Cracker, Cecil Aldin's bull terrier, became one of them in 1937: 'Cracker, the bull terrier, for many years the beloved companion and favourite model of the late Cecil Aldin, died July 31st, Mallorca. Deeply mourned'.

To understand how this arose, one must appreciate the popularity of Cecil Aldin, undoubtedly one of the supreme illustrators of the dog. Working in the early decades of the twentieth century, he was responsible for well over sixty books. He drew dogs from life, calling his own dog models 'The Professionals' and any visiting dogs he drew 'The Amateurs'. Cracker was his favourite model – immediately recognisable by his almost pure white coat and rakish black patch above his left eye. Together with Micky, an enormous Irish wolfhound, the two dogs featured in newspapers, magazines and many books, such as *Dogs of Character* (1927) and *Sleeping Partners* (1929). The reading public could not get enough of the doggy characters: Micky typically pictured sprawled across a sofa with Cracker trying to find a comfortable spot nearby – either in a corner of the sofa or, more usually, lying on top of his enormous friend.

Aldin loved illustrating mongrels as much as pure breeds. One of his most successful books was *A Dog Day or The Angel in the House* (1902), written by Walter Emanuel. It tells, in his own words, the story of a mongrel who accidentally disturbs a burglar and becomes a hero for the day. The story's charm comes from the wonderfully accurate pictures and honest descriptions of doggy – and human – behaviour.

Opposite: HAVING EATEN 'A WHOLE DISH OF MAYONNAISE FISH', THERE ARE UNSURPRISINGLY 'CURIOUS PAINS IN MY UNDERNEATH'.
From *A Dog Day or The Angel in the House* by Walter Emanuel, illustrated by Cecil Aldin.
William Heinemman, 1902

A Dog Day became one of the bestselling books of the period. Over 100,000 copies were sold between 1902 and the outbreak of the First World War in 1914, by which time Aldin's work was in constant demand, both for children and adults. As well as his dog illustrations he painted hunting scenes, and also illustrated several very popular books on country inns, old manor houses, and the cathedrals and churches of England. But it is for his dog illustrations that he is most admired, capturing the timeless sense of joy that exists between the dog and its owner.

Above: Cracker and Micky, Aldin's most famous dogs
From *Dogs of Character* written and illustrated by Cecil Aldin.
Eyre and Spottiswoode, 1927

Opposite: Snip and Snap, the twin spaniel puppies, find a rabbit
From *The Twins* written and illustrated by Cecil Aldin. Hodder & Stoughton, 1910

"Woof!" barked Timmy and leapt down to the platform almost on top of Dick

Timmy

The appeal of a story in which a group of young children set out on their own to solve mysteries and confront robbers, pirates and other perils is not unique. What distinguishes Enid Blyton's *Famous Five* is the fact that one of their gang, Timmy, is a dog. Timmy played as big a part in solving their mysteries as any of his companions, and he has remained equally popular with the generations of readers who have devoured these stories since the first was published in 1942.

Blyton only intended to write six to eight stories in the series. Its commercial success was so great, however, that she continued to write a *Famous Five* story every year (each story took her about four days to write) until 1962. Today over two million copies of the series are sold annually in over ninety countries.

Timmy the dog, the fifth member of the *Famous Five*, is introduced early on in the first story *Five on a Treasure Island* as George's dog. At first referred to rather formally as Timothy, he is described as 'a big brown mongrel ... He was the wrong shape, his head was too big, his ears were too pricked, his tail was too long and it was quite impossible to say what kind of dog he was supposed to be'.

The original illustrations were by Eileen Soper, an established wildlife artist much respected by Enid Blyton, who had written several nature guides for children. Timmy appears exactly as he is described, and Soper's pictures have a natural fluidity and sense of movement. In later editions other artists were used to create a more contemporary feel. These did not always draw on the text very accurately, and Timmy even appears as a border collie – a breed renowned for its intelligence, but surely not what Enid Blyton had intended.

Opposite: TIMMY THE MONGREL LEAPS ENTHUSIASTICALLY OUT OF A TRAIN
From *Five Have a Wonderful Time* by Enid Blyton, illustrated by Eileen Soper.
Hodder & Stoughton, 1952

Snoopy

FROM *Peanuts*

Yesterday I was a dog. Today I'm a dog. Tomorrow I'll probably still be a dog. Sigh! There's so little hope for advancement.

Snoopy the beagle is one of the cast of characters in the Peanuts comic strip. Artist Charles M Schulz first drew Snoopy as an unnamed dog in the weekly cartoon 'Li'l Folks', which he had devised in 1947 on his return home from service in the Second World War. These single-panel cartoons ran in his local paper, the St Paul Pioneer Press, featuring a girl named Patty, a boy called Charlie Brown and a dog that looked very much like Snoopy. 'Li'l Folks' was dropped after two years, but was picked up by the United Feature syndicate, first appearing as a cartoon strip on 2 October 1950. It was renamed 'Peanuts', the syndicate deciding that the rival comic strip 'Li'l Abner' was too similar in name. Schulz himself hated the Peanuts name, and it is significant that none of the printed books of the comic strips have the word 'Peanuts' within the title. Snoopy himself first appeared in the third strip on 4 October 1950, to be first identified by name on 10 November.

Snoopy began life as a conventional pet. He lived in a kennel (or doghouse), walked on four legs and was silent for the first two years of the comic strip. Only in 1952 did he start to 'speak' via thought balloons – a method of communication fortunately understood by his cartoon companions, and the one that he used from then on. As the comic strip grew more popular, Snoopy's anthropomorphism extended to walking on two legs, while his personality also became more complex. In an essay entitled 'The Americanisation of Augustine', cultural historian Arthur Asa Berger described Snoopy as 'an existential hero in every sense of the term' – a dog who 'strives, with dogged persistence and unyielding courage, to overcome what seems to be his fate – that he is a dog'.

By the 1960s Snoopy was regularly stealing the show every time he appeared. In 1965 he famously imagined himself as a flying ace of the First World War, battling the Red Baron and using his kennel as a Sopwith Camel (the British single-seat fighter biplane). The image went on to be reproduced many times, including as postage stamps, by the military and in music. The 1967 song 'Snoopy's Christmas', in which Snoopy and the Red Baron declare a truce on Christmas Eve, was based on the real event that took place in 1914 between British and German soldiers on the Western Front.

Over the years Snoopy's character and interests have developed in other ways. As well as his interest in history he is athletic, playing ice hockey, tennis and basketball. He is literate, although admits to reading *War and Peace* at a rate of one word per day. Efforts as a novelist have so far been largely unsuccessful, perhaps because every book he writes starts with the words, 'It

was a dark and stormy night...' He is a superb dancer, performing the 'Happy Snoopy' dance at suppertime, and adept at playing the accordion. One of the few areas in which he has never excelled in is love, and every romantic encounter leaves him broken hearted.

Schulz was pragmatic about the brand licensing of Snoopy and other Peanuts characters, declaring that, 'The strip is a commercial product to begin with. Comic strips sell newspapers. That's what they are there for.' When Schulz died in 2000 he had written 17,897 comic strips, which continue to appear in over 2,200 newspapers, in 75 countries and 25 languages. Snoopy's appeal as an instantly recognisable cultural icon was summed up by Schulz: 'Some comic strip characters, just like in any other media, sort of rise above what they are ... Popeye is immortal. Mickey Mouse is immortal. Charlie Chaplin. I think Snoopy has done that too'.

the Cadpig felt just a bit envious—but she was happy
to know she had grown too strong to need any cart.

The white Persian Cat, who was now a charming
creature (kindness makes kind cats) was extremely
gracious to the farmyard tabby. It was the beginning of
a firm friendship.

At last the motor-coach drove in through the wide
open gates of Hell Hall. The pond now reflected a snow-

101 Dalmatians

One of the reasons we know so much about the writer Dodie Smith is because she kept extensive journals. On 16 December 1954, for example, she wrote that she had read a book by Enid Blyton for the first time, and immediately afterwards decided that she too would write a book for children.

At that time Smith was an established writer, best known for some rather brittle and mannered plays, then somewhat out of favour, and for her novel *I Capture the Castle*, published six years earlier. That December night she sat and worked until 3 a.m. as the story gathered shape. She knew that it would be about dalmatians, a breed she had kept for over twenty years, and it was the memory of the first litter of fifteen puppies, hand-delivered by herself and her husband, that she drew upon to plot the story of the 101 *Dalmatians*.

The idea of the villainess, Cruella de Vil, derived from the remark of an actress friend who saw Smith's first dalmation, Pongo, as a puppy and declared that 'he would make a nice fur coat'. The image stuck in her mind, inspiring a plot in which an evil woman would steal dalmatian puppies in order to start a puppy farm. Pongo was cast as a canine Sherlock Holmes, on a mission to locate the stolen puppies and return them home to their owners.

The finished novel was bought by the publishers William Heinemann for a £100 advance, with royalties due to escalate when sales exceeded 7500 copies. Originally Smith had wanted Edward Ardizzone to illustrate the book, but he declined. The task was given instead to Janet and Anne Grahame-Johnstone, passionate animal lovers who spent many hours perfecting their

Opposite: Mr and Mrs Dearly, surrounded by their dalmations
From *One Hundred and One Dalmations* by Dodie Smith,
illustrated by Janet and Anne Grahame-Johnstone. William Heinemann, 1956

drawings of dalmatians. They worked from life for many of the human characters; for example the husband of Cruella de Vil was based on a furrier seen on the 1950s British television quiz show 'What's My Line?'.

The 101 Dalmatians was published on 19 November 1956, priced at ten shillings and sixpence. It proved a great success; everyone loved it. *The Times Literary Supplement* commended it as 'a doggy tale that will please a great many children, so light it is, so sentimental, so well-illustrated, so easy to read with not one slow word in its expert telling'. The author and critic John Rowe Townsend observed that, 'If dogs could read they would be unable to put it down'.

Less than three months later Disney asked to purchase film rights. The contract was signed in a matter of months, although production of the film took rather longer, costing four million dollars over three years and involving a team of 300 artists.

At the London preview in 1961 the audience included a beautifully behaved dalmatian in the front row, who apparently never took his eyes off the screen. The reviews were magnificent, and Disney was seen to have returned to form after its less successful predecessor, a cartoon of *The Sleeping Beauty*. The bandwagon was rolling, with doggy merchandise and spin-off books, although Smith's own sequel *The Starlight Barking*, published in 1965, was not so well received.

Dodie Smith died in 1990, and so never witnessed the re-release of the film in 1991, which grossed $66 million. Nor did she see the remake in 1996 which famously combined human characters with live puppies – something that would surely have delighted her.

Above: NINETY-SEVEN DALMATIONS AT HELL HALL
From *One Hundred and One Dalmations* by Dodie Smith, illustrated by Janet and Anne Grahame-Johnstone. William Heinemman, 1956

Dogmatix

FROM *Asterix*

The year is 50 BC and Gaul is entirely occupied by the Romans. Well, not entirely. One small village of indomitable Gauls still holds out against the invaders.

Fast forward 2000 years, to an era when the world has been entirely conquered by reality television rejects and fast food. Well, not entirely. One indomitable corner of French literature still holds out against the invaders. Asterix the Gaul, his colossal sidekick Obelix and their tiny dog Dogmatix gently continue to prod fun at national stereotypes and pun their way through adventures. Created by Albert Uderzo, who drew the cartoons, and René Goscinny, who wrote the original stories, Asterix first appeared in a comic strip in the magazine *Pilote* in 1959.

Dogmatix's first appearance came in the fifth story in the series, *Asterix and the Banquet*, serialised in *Pilote* in 1963 and published in book format in 1965. He is first seen at the beginning of the story in the door of a butcher's shop in Lutetia, and then

pops up in almost every panel. Dogmatix is not acknowledged until the very final scene, however, when he barks; Obelix pats him on the head and gives him a bone.

The little white dog of unknown breed was very popular with readers of *Pilote*, and a competition was devised to find him a name. A number of suggestions included 'Patracourcix' (*pattes raccourcis* or *short legs*) or 'Papeurdurix' (*pas peur du risque* or *not afraid of risk*), Trépetix and Paindépix, but Goscinny and Uderzo decided on the shorter name of 'Idéfix'. This is the name by which the little dog is known in most of the world, the exceptions being editions in Afrikaans, where is known as Woofix, and the English language versions where he is Dogmatix. This ingenious name came from the English translators, Anthea Bell and Derek Hockridge, whose creativity in finding new names for the French characters has been a large part of the books' success. In a 2009 interview Anthea Bell explained: 'If you are faithful to the spirit in translation then you have to be free with the letter – fidelity to the spirit is what matters. We and the French like the humour of historical anachronism. We have a lot of history behind us and we like to laugh at it in both nations'.

From the fifth story on, Dogmatix accompanied Asterix and Obelix on all their adventures. He rarely played a pivotal role in the plots, although in *Asterix and Cleopatra* he prevented Asterix and Obelix from being entombed in a pyramid. He was also an early champion of environmental concerns, howling whenever a tree was damaged. Dogmatix's popularity resulted in a series of

Opposite: From *Asterix and Cleopatra* by René Goscinny,
illustrated by Albert Uderzo. Hachette, 1965,
English edition published Hodder & Stoughton, 1969

spin-off books in the 1970s, but these are no longer in print.

In 1974 Goscinny and Uderzo created Les Studios Idéfix to produce their animated film, *The Twelve Tasks of Asterix* (Dogmatix appears as a canine version of the Metro Goldwyn Mayer lion). There are seven or eight feature-length cartoon films, and three live-action films in which Dogmatix is played by a variety of breeds, including a West Highland terrier (with dyed ears). The adventures of Asterix and his companions have been translated into 107 languages and have sold 350 million copies worldwide; there is even an Asterix theme park. 'By Toutatis!' (as Obelix would say), the indomitable Gauls have had the last laugh.

Above: From *Asterix and the Banquet* by René Goscinny,
illustrated by Albert Uderzo.
Hachette, 1965, English edition published Hodder & Stoughton, 1979

Spot the Dog

The self-styled 'world's favourite puppy' was created by Eric Hill in 1978 in response to his two-year-old son's demands for a bedtime story – as so many stories for children are. Hill had trained as a graphic designer in the art department of an advertising agency, but had always produced cartoons in his spare time. He particularly liked drawing planes, a legacy of his time in the RAF during the Second World War. He admits that the markings on an aircraft had a direct influence on his visualisation of Spot, who has spots on his body and on the tip of his tail. The conception of a puppy as the central character was a natural one: 'I have always been a "dog man" so it was quite natural for me to create a canine character who would be as playful and endearing as the real thing'.

Hill had been working on an advertisement involving the use of a lift-the-flap picture, and he noticed that his young son was captivated by the idea of a secret picture, hidden behind the hinged flap on the page. So he devised the first in a long line of

stories about Spot, a beagle puppy, and his friends. Each tale included the new interactive lift-the-flap device, designed for children's small hands to lift up and discover a new picture to add to the story. The first book, *Where's Spot*, was published in 1980, and although Hill says that he had no intention of it being a published work when he designed the story, the concept was an immediate success: 'I am quite convinced now...that the actual training of drawing cartoons – which is, of course, my style – led to my producing Spot. Cartoons must be very simple and have as few words as possible and so too must the Spot books'.

More quirky stories followed, each one featuring Spot and his friends in situations recognisable to an international readership. The distinctive typeface of the books, a variety of Century Schoolbook known as Infant, is very rarely used but offers a perfect medium for the simple narrative style.

Opposite and below: SPOT AND HIS MOTHER SALLY
From *Spot the Dog*, written and illustrated by Eric Hill. Heinemann, 1980

Hairy Maclary

FROM *Donaldson's Dairy*

Hairy Maclary from Donaldson's Dairy,
Hercules Morse as big as a horse,
Bottomley Potts covered in spots,
Muffin McLay like a bundle of hay,
Bitzer Maloney all skinny and bony,
Schnitzel von Krumm with a very low tum.

Hairy Maclary is the mischievous leader of a gang of dogs in Lynley Dodd's series of picture books. He is a cross-bred terrier, as she explains: 'The mongrel mix seemed perfect for an entertaining tale because terriers are cheeky, springy legged and confident. I'd planned for a hairy dog and needed a name that rhymed ... Maclary seemed fun and had the right number of syllables'.

The first Hairy Maclary book, published in 1983, came about almost by accident. 'I keep an ideas book with all sorts of silly snippets and snatches of verse', Dodd says. 'As I opened it, out fell a page on which I'd sketched a little terrier three years beforehand, with four lines of verse'. It was to become the basis of *Hairy Maclary from Donaldson's Dairy*.

All the dogs in the books are observed from life, and their mischievous ways will strike a chord with every dog owner – sniffing around lamp posts, barking at birds, scavenging in litter bins and pulling on leads.

Hairy Maclary now has ten books of his own. Their appeal lies in the mix of lively illustrations with clever language, perfectly paced in rhyme and metre. Dodd explains, 'I'm never satisfied with second best and even today do up to twenty-two drafts'.

Opposite: HAIRY MACLARY AND FRIENDS GO FOR A WALK AS SCARFACE CLAW
THE CAT PEERS OUT FROM BEHIND A FENCE
From *Hairy Maclary from Donaldson's Dairy*, by Lynley Dodd. Spindlewood, 1983

Blue Dog

The first appearance of Blue Dog was in a book of ghost stories entitled *Bayou*, in 1984. Louisiana artist George Rodrigue had been approached to provide forty paintings to illustrate the stories, inspired by regional myths and culture. Rather than follow the specific details of each story, he drew on their themes and titles to create the paintings, the most famous of which is the illustration for 'Slaughter House'. This tale of a ghost dog who guarded a house is taken from a Cajun myth of the *Loup Garou* – a strange dog (or werewolf) who haunted cemeteries and sugar cane fields and whose name was invoked by mothers as a threat to naughty children. The shape and stance of the Blue Dog figure was inspired by Rodrigue's own terrier-spaniel, Tiffany, who had died a few years earlier.

The dog in the first *Loup Garou* painting sits with an uncanny stillness before the haunted house. His blue coat contrasts with the red of the house and the white tombstone steps linking the two subjects. As if to underline his otherworldly presence, his yellow eyes stare out unflinchingly at the viewer. There is nothing malevolent about Blue Dog. In this and every other painting, his solid stance and questioning doggy expression make an instant connection with the viewer – which, like all great art, continues to resonate long afterwards.

Why is he blue? As Rodrigue says: 'An artist has to have a lot of guts and do things and take chances that might not make sense to the art world at the time. There was a risk factor that was very prevalent in everything I saw ... My decision to ... paint something from the past with contemporary eyes, to me, took guts ... I can't tell you how many people told me I was crazy, I was

Opposite: THE ORIGINAL IMAGE OF BLUE DOG IN FRONT OF A HAUNTED HOUSE
Watchdog, oil on canvas. George Rodrigue, 1984

stupid, I would ruin my art career. Why would I paint this when my Cajun paintings were selling and I made a good living? Once the public got to know the Blue Dog, the next round of comments was, "Yeah, but this will only last three or four years. What are you going to do next?"'

What Rodrigue did next was to paint dozens more Blue Dogs – deceptively simple images appearing within blocks of rich colours and strong shapes, yet always rooted in the cultural iconography of contemporary America. A major book deal led to the publication of *Blue Dog* in 1994, and the book went on to sell more than 200,000 copies – a phenomenal achievement for an expensive, heavyweight art book. Nine more books for adults and children followed. Rodrigue has been cautious in his use of the Blue Dog image, and it is rarely licensed for commercial use. The only means of viewing Blue Dog's image is, with few exceptions, through books and paintings. Despite his international fame Rodrigue still remains firmly connected to his culture and community. He raises money through the Blue Dog Relief Fund (which has to date raised nearly $3.5 million) and the George Rodrigue Foundation of the Arts, which promotes education in the arts.

Opposite: 'ARE YOU LONESOME TONIGHT'
original silkscreen. George Rodrigue, 2009

The King's Fire Dogs

Animals are a regular part of folk stories around the world. A folk tale from Korea typically portrays dogs as loyal and brave, but ultimately foolish creatures.

The story goes that a king lived in a heavenly kingdom that was always in darkness. He was desperate to bring light into his kingdom, so he sent one of his fiercest dogs, from a breed known as Fire Dogs, to steal the Sun. The Fire Dog tried to seize the Sun in its mouth, but it was too hot. He snapped at it again and again, but in the end had to give up and return without his prey. The king then turned to his next Fire Dog and sent him to the Moon, but when that Fire Dog tried to bite the Moon, it froze in his mouth. He, too, had to spit it out and return without his prize. It is said in Korea that this is how the eclipses of the Sun and Moon are caused; the parts that the Fire Dogs bit are the parts darkened during the eclipse.

Contemporary illustrator Jane Ray beautifully portrays the king surrounded by his elegant Fire Dogs, possibly greyhounds or salukis. Several of the dogs gaze up at the moon through the window, looking wistfully at what they can never have.

Opposite: THE KING AND HIS FIRE DOGS LOOK UP AT THE MOON
From *Sun, Moon and Stars* by Mary Hoffman, illustrated by Jane Ray.
Orion Publishing Group, 1998